This book belongs to: _____

Start Date: _____

# a guide to a better you

## 20 TRANSFORMATIVE QUESTIONS TO DEEPEN YOUR FAITH AND CHANGE YOUR LIFE

## JOE CARTER

ZONDERVAN®

ZONDERVAN

*A Guide to a Better You*

Portions of this book were excerpted from the *NIV Lifehacks Bible: Practical Tools for Successful Spiritual Habits.*

Published in Grand Rapids, Michigan, by Zondervan. Zondervan is a registered trademark of HarperCollins Christian Publishing, Inc.

Requests for information should be addressed to customercare@harpercollins.com.

Scripture quotations are taken from the Holy Bible, New International Version®, NIV®. Copyright © 1973, 1978, 1984, 2011 by Biblica, Inc.® Used by permission of Zondervan. All rights reserved worldwide. www.Zondervan.com. The "NIV" and "New International Version" are trademarks registered in the United States Patent and Trademark Office by Biblica, Inc.®

Any internet addresses (websites, blogs, etc.) and telephone numbers in this book are offered as a resource. They are not intended in any way to be or imply an endorsement by Zondervan, nor does Zondervan vouch for the content of these sites and numbers for the life of this book.

Cover design: Jamie DeBruyn
Interior design: Emily Ghattas

ISBN 978-0-310-15252-1 (softcover)

*Printed in Malaysia*
24 25 26 27 28 29  COS  6 5 4 3 2 1

# Contents

# Introduction

***A Guide to a Better You*** is a compilation of practical advice on the most important journey you'll ever take. It's a toolkit for restructuring your life so that you can become more like Jesus. Each section focuses on a trait that will help you become a better person.

I'm not an expert, but in my own attempt to discover what I should do to become more like Jesus, I've stumbled across insights and wisdom from hundreds of men and women who can help you grow in grace and Christlikeness.

# How to Use This Book

Read the entry. Highlight words, phrases, or Scripture references that speak to you. Take notes in the margins.

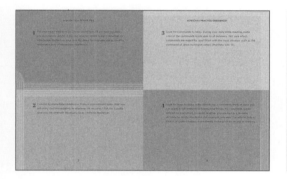

Respond to the reflection prompts. If you're completing this workbook as a group, you can write down additional thoughts people share.

After you've completed a section, record how everything is going. This will serve as a check-in with yourself and help you progress on your journey to being the best version of yourself.

# How Can I Practice Obedience?

## READ: GENESIS 6:22

**The Bible mentions many people** whose obedience to God came from their faith and love for Him (Hebrews 11). For example, Abel offered a more excellent sacrifice (Genesis 6:4); Abraham left Ur at God's direction, not knowing his destination (v. 8); and Moses refused the privileges of being called Pharaoh's son, choosing rather to identify with Israel, God's people (vv. 24–25)[1]. In each case their faith motivated their action.

> **Noah provides an example not only of obedience but of immediate surrender and faithfulness.**

One of the most astounding exemplars of faith in action was Noah. God tells Noah to build an ark and stock it with animals, and "Noah did everything just as God commanded him" (Genesis 6:22). Noah provides an example not only of obedience but of immediate obedience.

Here are five ways to begin practicing immediate obedience in your own life:

**1** Fill your heart with love for Christ. Jesus said, "If you love me, keep my commands" (John 14:15). Our love for Christ is our motivation for obedience. Reflect on your love for Jesus to motivate you to want to undertake acts of immediate obedience.

**2** Commit to immediate obedience. Make a commitment today that you will obey God immediately in whatever He requires.[2] Ask the Lord to give you the strength necessary to act without hesitation.

**3** Look for commands to obey. During your daily Bible reading, make a list of the commands applicable to all believers. Not sure which commands are meant for you? Start with the most obvious, such as the command of Jesus to forgive others (Matthew 6:14–15).

**4** Look for ways to obey. After identifying a command, think of ways you can apply it within the next twenty-four hours. If a command seems difficult to implement, consider whether you are facing a genuine obstacle to timely obedience (for example, you won't be able to help a widow or orphan today) or are merely looking for an excuse to disobey.

**5** Look for unique opportunities. If you come across a specific command in your daily Scripture reading, be watchful for unique circumstances God might provide for you to obey. Have a plan for obedience, but be open, ready, and willing to obey in whatever ways God provides.

| MONTH | DAY | YEAR |
|:-:|:-:|:-:|
| ⬤ | ⬤ | ⬤ |

**GOD SIGHTINGS**

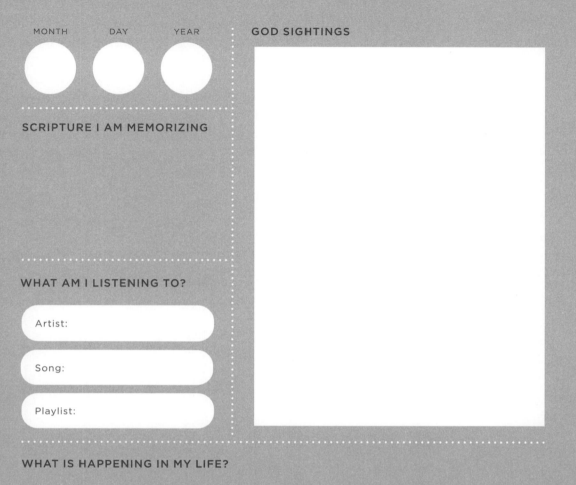

**SCRIPTURE I AM MEMORIZING**

**WHAT AM I LISTENING TO?**

Artist:

Song:

Playlist:

**WHAT IS HAPPENING IN MY LIFE?**

**WHAT IS HAPPENING IN THE WORLD?**

# How Can I Develop Persistence?

## READ: GENESIS 32

**In one of the Bible's strangest tales,** Jacob physically wrestles with God. Jacob was headed home to face his brother Esau, whom he hadn't seen in the twenty years since Esau wronged him (Genesis 32:4). Although Jacob had reached out to God for help, he was still resisting fully submitting to his will. That's when God confronted him face-to-face.

The wrestling match lasted throughout the night, and yet Jacob wouldn't let go. God crippled Jacob's hip, and Jacob still wouldn't let go. He remained persistent throughout the great struggle and refused to let go until God blessed him. Because Jacob acknowledged God as the

**Persistence doesn't require overcoming every difficulty; it merely requires that you refuse to give up.**

7

source of the blessings, the Lord honored his request. Through this account, we see Jacob coming to a point of true faith.

In his commentary on this passage, Kurt Strassner writes,

Here is a reminder that undergoing the great change—becoming a Christian—is not always quick and easy. It is not just a matter of repeating a prayer, making a decision, or filling out a card. True conversion often comes only after intense wrestling with God. A new identity in Jesus often comes only after a period of persistently praying like Jacob, "I will not let you go unless you bless me."[1]

Want to cultivate persistence that rivals Jacob's? Check out these three ways to prepare:

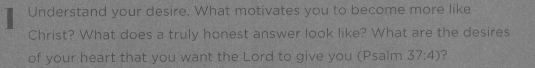

1  Understand your desire. What motivates you to become more like Christ? What does a truly honest answer look like? What are the desires of your heart that you want the Lord to give you (Psalm 37:4)?

**2** Outline your steps. Persistence in your journey will come easier when you understand what you need to do next. What are the next steps? How are you fine-tuning your choices to make spiritual formation integral to your daily routine?

**3** Expect difficulties. At some point during his struggle, Jacob realized that while he couldn't overcome the stranger, he could at least hang on. Then the stranger did something unexpected and made "the socket of Jacob's hip so that his hip was wrenched" (Genesis 32:25). At that point, the pain was likely overwhelming, and Jacob was surely ready to concede. Yet he refused to give up.

Persistence doesn't require overcoming every difficulty; it merely requires that you refuse to give up. It is through such difficulties that God strengthens your character. Difficulties are inevitable, so be prepared. You don't have to foresee the challenges you'll face to know that if you refuse to give up, you can endure. Hang on until God blesses you.

MONTH    DAY    YEAR

GOD SIGHTINGS

SCRIPTURE I AM MEMORIZING

WHAT AM I LISTENING TO?

Artist:

Song:

Playlist:

WHAT IS HAPPENING IN MY LIFE?

WHAT IS HAPPENING IN THE WORLD?

# What Does and Does Not Require Forgiveness?

## READ: GENESIS 45:4–7

**Joseph had a solid reason** for wanting revenge against his brothers: they planned to kill him but instead sold him into slavery and told his parents he had died. And then, to his surprise, their paths crossed again. Now Joseph was in a position of power and authority; he could have had his brothers executed or sold as slaves. Instead, he forgave them (Genesis 45:4–7).

Joseph understood that God had used the crime to save the lives of others (v. 5). But knowing God used the situation for good probably didn't remove all of Joseph's hurt and pain. Forgiveness is necessary, but it isn't always easy. Knowing what is and is not required of us can help us through the process of forgiving those who have wronged us.

Forgiveness requires many layers:

- Understand what it is: Forgiveness is a decision and a promise to release a person by canceling the real debt the person has with you.[1] It's returning to God the right to take care of justice.[2]

- Focus on how God has forgiven you: The starting point of our willingness and ability to forgive is God's forgiveness of our sins. Reflect on the many ways you have sinned against your Creator, then think about the price He paid so that you could be forgiven and restored. Focusing on your gratitude for what God has done in forgiving your sins often makes it easier to forgive the hurts caused by others.

- Accept that forgiveness is not optional: Gratitude to God will often motivate us to forgive others. But when the hurt and pain are too deep and forgiveness seems impossible, we might need to remind ourselves that forgiving others is not optional; it's a prerequisite for our own forgiveness. As Jesus said, "For if you forgive other people when they sin against you, your heavenly Father will also forgive you. But if you do not forgive others their sins, your Father will not forgive your sins" (Matthew 6:14–15).

- Separate your feelings from forgiveness: If you rely on your feelings to let you know when it is time to forgive, you might never do it. The time to forgive is always now, not when our feelings catch up or the hurt has passed.

- Realize psychological relief is not the reason: Often when we forgive someone who has wronged us, we will eventually feel a sense of relief or peace. While this is a welcome benefit of forgiveness, it is not the reason we forgive.

- Know that the initiative is on the forgiver: May we wait until someone seeks our forgiveness before we forgive them? No, we may not. Jesus expects us to forgive those who sin against us even before they request it or take responsibility for what they have done (Mark 11:25).

- Accept that forgiveness is an ongoing process: We tend to want a "once and for all" forgiveness event, but Jesus reminds us that with some people or situations, we will need to forgive over and over and over again (Matthew 18:21–22).

- Leave the past behind, but be wise moving forward: We can forgive without forgetting the situation that caused the debt. For instance, if someone has physically abused you in the past, you can forgive them without putting yourself into a situation where they can continue to harm you. Forgiveness might lead us to seek reconciliation, but we are not required to put ourselves in danger. As Rose Sweet says, "While God commands us to forgive others, he never told us to keep trusting those who violated our trust or even to like being around those who hurt us."[3]

- Have a face-to-face meeting or restoration of relationship with the offender: Aaron Sironi explains:

Though we are called to forgive those who sin against us, and we must be ready and willing to do so (attitudinal forgiveness), pursuing relational reconciliation is complex and not automatic. As a general rule, if the offender has not repented, has not acknowledged the sin, and does not ask for forgiveness (transactional forgiveness), reconciliation is not warranted. The decision to reconcile is also impacted by the duration and severity of the sin involved.[4]

How have your views on forgiveness changed? How will you now approach the process?

MONTH    DAY    YEAR

GOD SIGHTINGS

SCRIPTURE I AM MEMORIZING

WHAT AM I LISTENING TO?

Artist:

Song:

Playlist:

WHAT IS HAPPENING IN MY LIFE?

WHAT IS HAPPENING IN THE WORLD?

# What Steps Can I Take to Break Negative Habits?

## READ: EXODUS 16

**After the exodus out of Egypt,** the Hebrews' lives were upended. While many aspects of their previous lives had been harsh, they missed others, such as knowing where their next meal would come from.

Like all humans, the Hebrew people were creatures of habit. So God changed their behavior in the desert by forcing them to develop habits of trust in his provision (Exodus 16:4–5). Habits drive our behavior, which in turn forms our character. This is why understanding how to make and break habits is such an important skill for spiritual formation.

For our purposes, we can classify habits into four broad categories: positive, negative, virtuous, and sinful. Positive habits improve our lives in a general way (brushing our teeth), while virtuous habits make us more Christlike (prayer and Scripture reading). Both types are formed using the same method.

Negative habits generally have negative effects on our lives (eating junk food), while sinful habits lead us away from God and to our destruction. How we deal with these two types of habits is quite different, so we'll consider sinful habits separately.

Following are six steps to help break negative habits:

1 Identify your own negative habits: While some negative habits are bad for anyone, the effects on many others vary from person to person. For example, staying up too late at night might be a negative habit if you have to wake up early, and it prevents you from getting enough sleep. But for other people, staying up late might be a benefit because it allows them to get more done at a time of day when there are fewer distractions. To identify your own negative habits, make a list of the recurring troubles in your life, then identify patterns of behavior that might cause or contribute to the problem.

**2** Isolate the habit loop: Every habit, positive or negative, starts with a behavioral pattern called a "habit loop." This loop consists of three parts: a cue, routine, and reward. The cue is a type of trigger that tells your brain to go into automatic mode and begin the routine, which is the behavior itself. The final step is the reward, an internal or external stimulus that satisfies your brain and helps it remember the habit loop.[1]

**3** Change the trigger: Some negative habits can be overcome simply by changing the trigger. Take, for example, the negative habit of checking your email when you are trying to engage in another activity, such as Bible reading. The cue for this habit is likely some sort of notification (either visual or audio) that you have a new email. Negative habits generally have negative effects on our lives (such as eating junk food), while sinful habits lead us away from God and to our destruction. This triggers the behavior (checking your email) that your brain has been conditioned to reward (the brain likes novelty, and reading an email temporarily satisfies your curiosity). By simply turning off such notifications, you can remove the trigger that activates the behavior.

**4** Modify the context: Along with the three parts of the habit loop, negative habits also tend to include a strong contextual element. Specifically, we are more likely to engage in negative habits when we are bored, stressed, or seeking to avoid an activity (such as procrastinating from work).

**5** Replace the negative habit with a positive one: Eliminating negative habits is extremely difficult. But the process can be much easier if we simply replace the habit with a better one. Once you've identified the negative habit, consider how you can "reengineer" the habit loop to replace the negative habit with a more positive routine.

**6** Plan for setbacks: Negative habits are difficult to overcome. Expect that it will take numerous attempts and lots of trial and error before you are able to replace a negative habit with one that aids in your flourishing. Ask God to give you the strength and ability to persevere.

MONTH   DAY   YEAR

GOD SIGHTINGS

SCRIPTURE I AM MEMORIZING

WHAT AM I LISTENING TO?

Artist:

Song:

Playlist:

WHAT IS HAPPENING IN MY LIFE?

WHAT IS HAPPENING IN THE WORLD?

# What Is the Essential Vocation of Burden Bearing?

## READ: EXODUS 18:13-27

**Next time you feel overwhelmed** by your obligations, consider what it must have been like for Moses. For the ancient Israelites, Moses served as the chief leader, primary lawgiver (delivering God's laws) and sole judge in disputes.

When Jethro, Moses' father-in-law, heard about these duties, he offered wise insight: "What you are doing is not good. You and these people who come to you will only wear yourselves out. The work is too heavy for you; you cannot handle it alone" (Exodus 18:17–18). Jethro recommended appointing other capable and trustworthy men to be judges. As he said, "That will make your load lighter, because they will share it with you" (v. 22).

**For Christians, helping to share one another's burdens is not just good advice; it's a way we fulfill the law of Christ.**

For Christians, helping to share one another's burdens is not just good advice; it's a way we fulfill the law of Christ

(Galatians 6:2). Commenting on this command, John Piper says,

> Some of you wonder what you are supposed to do with your life. Here is a vocation that will bring you more satisfaction than if you became a millionaire ten times over: Develop the extraordinary skill for detecting the burdens of others and devote yourself daily to making them lighter.[1]

Here are three ways to hone the skill of burden bearing:

**1** Be watchful for indirect opportunities: In many cases, we can't bear others' burdens directly. We can't often take their place or do their tasks for them. We can, however, help them indirectly by reducing other strains and distractions in their life.

**2** Be willing to do small deeds: "So many of our good deeds are so small," says Tim Challies. "They seem paltry. Instead of handing over the keys to a brand-new car, we hand over a slightly overcooked casserole. Instead of funding an extreme makeover for that person's home, we show up on Saturday morning to help apply a new coat of paint."[2]

**3** Be ready for the boring: Burden-bearing is often boring. It's not exciting work that will garner you lots of attention. But it is absolutely essential work. Don't wait for a future time when you can be a hero; be a help right now.

How can you devote yourself daily to make the burdens of others lighter?

MONTH    DAY    YEAR

GOD SIGHTINGS

SCRIPTURE I AM MEMORIZING

WHAT AM I LISTENING TO?

Artist:

Song:

Playlist:

WHAT IS HAPPENING IN MY LIFE?

WHAT IS HAPPENING IN THE WORLD?

# How Can I Expose the Idols in My Life?

## READ: EXODUS 32

**Few stories in the Old Testament** tend to make us feel more superior to the Israelites than the tale of the golden calf (Exodus 32:1–6). How backward they must have been to think you could make a god out of metal. How silly they were to think taking offerings to this statue would bring them peace, joy, and happiness. The entire story is almost too absurd to believe. Or at least it is until we examine the idols in our modern-day life.

Imagine if the Israelites could see the idols we bow down before—big-screen TVs, grades on a report card, "likes" on social media. They would likely find our idols even more ridiculous than we find their golden calf.

The reason idolatry is condemned in the Ten Commandments is because idolatry is the core reason we ever do anything wrong. As Tim Keller notes, "We never break the other commandments without breaking the first one."[1] The secret to change, Keller adds, is always to identify and dismantle the basic idols of the heart.

Here are a few areas to examine to identify the idols in your own life. Not all of these will be idols, for there is much in creation that we have been given for our enjoyment. We can appreciate the gifts of God without making them a replacement for Him. But if they are the first things your mind turns to rather than to God, then you might have identified a problem area.

- Examine your imagination. What do you daydream about? When your mind wanders, is it to material goods, like a beautiful home and exotic vacations, or to intangible items, such as a successful career or the approval of your peers?

- Examine your attention. Consider the times when you would rather be doing something else other than practicing a spiritual discipline. What activity would you rather be doing instead? Do you regularly turn to one or more time-wasting activities when you want to avoid productive tasks?

- Examine your finances. Most of us have discretionary or disposable income, money left over after the bills have been paid. How do you spend your disposable income? What material goods or services are you most likely to go into debt to finance?

- Examine your prayer life. How often do you go to God in prayer? Do you pray primarily as a rote exercise or to ask God for things? Or do you gladly spend time in worship, reflection, and repentance? How do you feel when God doesn't respond to your prayers in the way you wanted Him to? Do you trust that He knows best, or do you become angry and bitter?

- Examine your relationships. What person do you love the most? What person in your life do you most want to please? Do you have friendships or romantic attachments that lead you away from God? Or are you so self-focused that you've lost sight of God and other people?

- Examine your emotions. What do you fear most? What do you most hope for? What are you most passionate about? What do you desire the most? What makes you extremely angry or sad?

- Examine your concerns. What do you worry about? What makes you most anxious? What do you most fear losing?

- Examine your past and future. What is one thing from your past that you would like to change? What makes you nostalgic? What are your biggest regrets? What do you most want to happen in the future? What would cause you to despair if it didn't come to pass?

Use these questions to uncover the deepest cravings and desires of your heart. Once you've identified a potential idol, consider whether you've put it ahead of or in place of God. Pray that God will help you become aware of your idols and then lead you on the long, hard path of faithfulness.

Like the Israelites, we might have to accept the bitter consequences of our idolatry. But any price is worth paying if it helps us to turn back to the true worship of Jesus.

MONTH     DAY     YEAR

SCRIPTURE I AM MEMORIZING

GOD SIGHTINGS

WHAT AM I LISTENING TO?

Artist:

Song:

Playlist:

WHAT IS HAPPENING IN MY LIFE?

WHAT IS HAPPENING IN THE WORLD?

# How Can Adjusting Cues Change My Behavior?

## READ: LEVITICUS 8

**Moses, directed by God,** consecrated Aaron and his sons for the priesthood. Consecration is the solemn dedication to a special purpose or service. Before they could engage in the behaviors of the priesthood, Aaron and his kin were treated to an elaborate set of consecration rituals (such as symbolic washing and priestly garments).

Although these actions were a form of behavior, they were also cues. Cues are signals or triggers that tell us to engage in a behavior. Of

**Because of the role cues play in changing behavior, it is helpful to understand how to use them to our advantage.**

the three things needed to come together for a behavior to occur—motivation, ability, and a cue—cues are often considered the least important. However, cues fulfill many important purposes, including serving as reminders, signaling when to begin a behavior, or, as in the case with the consecration ceremony, preparing us for future actions. Because of the role cues play in changing behavior, it is helpful to understand how to use them to our advantage.

Researchers have shown that almost all cues fit into one of five categories: location, time, emotional state, other people, and immediately preceding action.[1] Consider how each of these would affect a behavioral change.

Take, for instance, location. Where do you leave your house key? Most likely you leave it in the same location so when you leave home you are reminded to take it with you. When considering how to change a behavior, think about how it can be affected by location.

Whenever possible, we want to choose cues that take advantage of as many of these categories as possible. For instance, let's say you want to develop the habit of reading a devotion every day. To change your behavior and make the habit stick, you could include the following cues: after getting your morning coffee, sit down at the kitchen table (location and immediately preceding action) an hour before the rest of the family wakes up (time) when no one else is around (other people) and before you have to deal with the stresses of the day (emotional state). After a short time of following these cues, you should see results.

MONTH    DAY    YEAR

GOD SIGHTINGS

SCRIPTURE I AM MEMORIZING

WHAT AM I LISTENING TO?

Artist:

Song:

Playlist:

WHAT IS HAPPENING IN MY LIFE?

WHAT IS HAPPENING IN THE WORLD?

# SECTION 8

# How Can I Find My Place to Serve?

## READ: NUMBERS 2:34

*Where do I belong? What am I to do? How can I change the world?*

We tend to think of these as modern questions, but people have been asking them since the beginning of time. In earlier ages, though, the answers were often limited and easier to discover. For example, the twelve tribes of Israel were arranged in a way that allowed everyone in the community to know their place and how they would faithfully follow the commands of the Lord (Numbers 2:34). As R. Dennis Cole explains,

**Every community has people who need our help.**

The people of Israel were a community that had their essential meaning in relationship to God and to one another. But ever in the community was the continuing stress on the individual to know where he belonged in the larger grouping.[1]

41

We, too, find our essential meaning in relationship to God and to one another. Here are a few places we should look to help us discover how we as individuals can find our place to serve our communities:

- Look at your gifts: The first place we should look is to the specific gifts the Spirit gives us to build up the church. Every gift is important for building up the body of Christ. As Paul said, "There are different kinds of gifts, but the same Spirit distributes them. There are different kinds of service, but the same Lord" (1 Corinthians 12:4–5).
- Look at your resources: What resources do you have at your disposal? The resources we have can often be a clue to how we can serve. You might have transportation—whether a single bicycle or a fleet of semitrailer trucks—that helps you recognize the ability to deliver goods to those in need.
- Look at your context: The tribe of Simeon didn't have to go to the tribe of Asher to find neighbors to serve. Every community has people who need our help. God might lead us to help those far away, but He often puts us in a specific place so we can help those nearby. Our closest neighbors are often the ones we are called to serve.

Knowing what you now know about places to serve, how will you serve your community?

MONTH     DAY     YEAR

SCRIPTURE I AM MEMORIZING

WHAT AM I LISTENING TO?

Artist:

Song:

Playlist:

WHAT IS HAPPENING IN MY LIFE?

WHAT IS HAPPENING IN THE WORLD?

GOD SIGHTINGS

# How Can I Uncover Inadvertent Sins?

## READ: NUMBERS 35:9–34

**In this passage** we find God has set aside six of the Levitical cities to be designated as cities of refuge, places where a person who had committed manslaughter or caused some other form of unintentional death to an individual would be afforded asylum and protection from potential avenging by a member of the slain person's family. The manslayer had the responsibility of fleeing to the appointed city immediately after committing the crime so as to find refuge from the potential kinsman avenger.[1]

People guilty of unintentional or inadvertent sin could not afford to wait; they had to flee to a place where forgiveness could be obtained. In this way, the cities of refuge are representative of Christ, in whom sinners find a refuge from the destroyer of our souls. S. Michael Houdmann says, "Just as the guilty person sought refuge in the cities set up for that purpose, in the same way we flee to Christ for refuge from sin (Hebrews 6:18)."[2]

Here are seven questions to ask yourself to uncover inadvertent sins in your life.

**1** What person who has claimed I wronged them have I dismissed or ignored?

**2** Could I have sinned against them without intention?

**3** If so, how does Jesus want me to respond to them?

**4** James said, "If anyone, then, knows the good they ought to do and doesn't do it, it is sin for them" (James 4:17). How am I sinning by omission?

**5** What good should I have done this week but failed to do?

**6** In what ways am I most likely to unintentionally sin against God?

**7** Am I taking the time necessary to search His Word so that I might know His will and avoid offending Him?

By using these questions as a tool for self-reflection, you'll be less inclined to repeat your sins. Remember to ask Jesus to forgive these particular sins, and thank Him for being our never-failing refuge.

MONTH    DAY    YEAR

GOD SIGHTINGS

SCRIPTURE I AM MEMORIZING

WHAT AM I LISTENING TO?

Artist:

Song:

Playlist:

WHAT IS HAPPENING IN MY LIFE?

WHAT IS HAPPENING IN THE WORLD?

# How Can I Practice Solitude?

## READ: DEUTERONOMY 9:18

**Solitude is the discipline** that calls us to consciously pull away from everything else in our lives, including the company of other people, for the purpose of giving our full and undivided attention to God.[1] An exemplar of the practice was Moses. Throughout his life, Moses would often set himself apart to be alone with God, often for extended periods of time.

In Deuteronomy 9:18, Moses reminds the Israelites that he practiced solitude and fasting "before the Lord for forty days and forty nights" on their behalf. Such passages can make us uncomfortable and despairing of our own lack of discipline: Moses could spend forty days in solitude, yet we struggle to spend forty minutes alone with God! But with effort, we, too, can practice the discipline of solitude.

Here are three things to consider when practicing solitude:

> Commit to finding creative ways to be alone with God for extended periods of solitude, ranging from a few hours to a few days.

**1** Solitude doesn't require silence: Silence and solitude are complementary disciplines that aid our communion with God. But while silence almost always requires solitude, solitude does not necessarily require silence. We can use our time of solitude for prayer, verbal meditation on Scripture, singing psalms or hymns of praise or any other form of "noisy" activity. Solitude doesn't require either silence or a hushed solemnity.

**2** Solitude requires planning: Our lives tend to be filled with people and events, making it unlikely we'll accidentally stumble into solitude. Being alone with God requires planning. Choose a place where you can be intimate with God and free from distractions. This "special place" doesn't need to be special; it simply needs to be a place where you can remove yourself from the world for as much time as needed.

**3** Solitude requires time: On most days, the best we can do is to get away for a few minutes, or even an hour. We should cherish these times and guard them carefully. Yet while these solitary moments are necessary, they're hardly sufficient to meet our need for closeness with our Creator. Commit to finding creative ways to be alone with God for extended periods of solitude, ranging from a few hours to a few days.

Create your own plan for solitude.

MONTH   DAY   YEAR

GOD SIGHTINGS

SCRIPTURE I AM MEMORIZING

WHAT AM I LISTENING TO?

Artist:

Song:

Playlist:

WHAT IS HAPPENING IN MY LIFE?

WHAT IS HAPPENING IN THE WORLD?

# How Do I Build Connection Between Generations?

### READ: JUDGES 2:10

**God freed the Hebrews** from bondage and promised them a homeland of their own. The people, however, frequently ignored what God had done for them. Why were they often so faithless to a God who had been so faithful?

We find a primary reason in Judges 2:10: "After that whole generation had been gathered to their ancestors, another generation grew up who knew neither the LORD nor what he had done for Israel." As Daniel Isaac Bock explains, "The priests had failed in their instructional duties (Leviticus 10:11); and the elaborate system of festivals, memorials, and other customs, designed to pass on the rich spiritual tradition (Deuteronomy 6:20), had either lapsed or been reduced to formality."[1]

Whether in the home, community, or church, we lose an important part of the story of what God has done when there is a lack of fellowship and connection between generations. Here are three ways we can strengthen those connections:

**1** Seek out those from other generations: We often self-segregate by age groups, which requires that we make a concerted effort to seek out those who are younger or older than ourselves for fellowship. Make a list of your friends, combining them by broad age group (20s to 30s, 50s to 70s). Are age groups, whether younger or older, missing? How can you find ways to change that by making new connections?

**2** Speak and listen charitably: Our generational prejudices can cause us to be dismissive of those who are younger or older than us. To cultivate intergenerational friendships, we often need to be gracious and less critical, especially about cultural issues (such as musical taste) on which Christians have the freedom to disagree. Be charitable with those of other generations.

**3** Find the connection: As C. S. Lewis wrote, "Friendship is born at that moment when one man says to another: 'What! You too? I thought that no one but myself . . .'"[2] If we search, we can always find a connection with a fellow believer. And if nothing else, every Christian can, as Joseph Rhea says, stand beside every other and say, "You know Jesus too!? Tell me about it!"[3]

In your life, who would you like to build a better generational connection with? How will you do that?

MONTH     DAY     YEAR

**GOD SIGHTINGS**

**SCRIPTURE I AM MEMORIZING**

**WHAT AM I LISTENING TO?**

Artist:

Song:

Playlist:

**WHAT IS HAPPENING IN MY LIFE?**

**WHAT IS HAPPENING IN THE WORLD?**

# How Should I Handle Pressure?

## READ: JUDGES 2:10

**When we look closely** at the story of Israel, we find a recurring pattern. When the people are under pressure, they turn to God; when the pressure is off, "they forgot the LORD their God" (1 Samuel 12:9).

Pressure is a constraining or compelling force or influence in our lives. We can feel pressured by circumstances, other people, or even by God. It is this last type of pressure that often scares us the most. We know God only gives us what we need, but we resent the idea that what we need is *more* pressure. As Jon Bloom says, "Pressure is one of the more resented of God's graces."[1] Resented or not, we need to understand it.

> **We know God only gives us what we need, but we resent the idea that what we need is *more* pressure.**

- The purpose of pressure: If we want to make the muscles in our bodies stronger, there is only one way to accomplish the task: (1) apply increased loads (weights to our muscles until they are exhausted), (2) rest, and (3) repeat. This is the cycle by which pressure makes our bodies stronger. And it is also the way God makes us morally, mentally, and spiritually stronger.

- The difference between good and bad pressure: Not all types of pressure are created equal. Good pressure is that which forces us to rely on God and leads us to grow in faith. We might not like the process, but experiencing godly pressure and godly rest are how we're made stronger. Bad pressure is what we bring upon ourselves through sin, anxiety, or worry, often because we want to assume God's role. Rather than making us stronger, bad pressure breaks us down and makes us weaker.
- The benefits of pressure: Pressure has numerous benefits. As Jon Bloom explains,

> God only gives us the priceless grace of pressure so that we will share His holiness, bear the peaceful fruit of righteousness (Hebrews 12:10–11), exercise love for others (1 John 4:7), put their needs before ours (Philippians 2:3), and to push us toward Himself—our exceeding joy (Psalm 43:4).[2]

What pressure(s) are you experiencing? How can you better handle everything?

MONTH    DAY    YEAR

GOD SIGHTINGS

SCRIPTURE I AM MEMORIZING

WHAT AM I LISTENING TO?

Artist:

Song:

Playlist:

WHAT IS HAPPENING IN MY LIFE?

WHAT IS HAPPENING IN THE WORLD?

## SECTION 13

# How Can I Take Godly Criticism?

## READ: 1 SAMUEL 13:11–15

**Not many people have** the courage or authority to get away with criticizing a king. In ancient Israel, such rebuke could come from only one person: God's prophet. The Old Testament records two kings who had very different responses when they were rebuked.

Saul, impatient and fearful, overstepped his role and disobeyed God. Samuel rebuked the king, but there was no indication Saul was sorrowful about his actions or that he committed to atoning for his sin (1 Samuel 13:11–15). Compare that to the rebuke Nathan gave David. David heard the criticism and became immediately contrite: "Then David said to Nathan, 'I have sinned against the Lord'" (2 Samuel 12:13).

Both Nathan and Samuel gave the kings godly criticism, which Garrett Kell defines as "to give a corrective evaluation of another person and their service to the Lord with

71

the intent of helping that person grow in faithfulness to God."[1] Being able to graciously receive godly criticism is a mark of Christian maturity.

Here are four tips for how to do it well:

**1** Set aside your pride: No one likes to be criticized. But it becomes easier to take godly criticism when our desire to grow in spiritual maturity is greater than our need for prideful self-protection.

**2** Assume there is at least some truth in the criticism: "People are not infallible, so there are times their words of criticism or critique will be off-base and unwarranted," says Kell. "Your first response shouldn't be to shoot holes in what they are saying, but rather to see what bit of truth may be salvaged from their words. It's rare that you can't find a little gold in even the biggest load of trash."[2]

**3** Ask clarifying questions: Dig into the criticism by asking people to provide specific examples of the problem that needs to be fixed and ways you can improve.

**4** Be thankful for the criticism: If a brother or sister in Christ offers criticism that is warranted, thank both God and them for the rebuke and correction. While it might have been painful to hear, it will benefit your growth and likely have a positive impact on others.

List criticism that you've recently received. Reread the four tips for addressing criticism, then write down how you can put each tip into action.

**GOD SIGHTINGS**

**SCRIPTURE I AM MEMORIZING**

**WHAT AM I LISTENING TO?**

Artist:

Song:

Playlist:

**WHAT IS HAPPENING IN MY LIFE?**

**WHAT IS HAPPENING IN THE WORLD?**

# What Simple Questions Should I Ask?

## READ: 2 SAMUEL 21:2–4

**Every day we are required** to make thousands of decisions. Researchers at Cornell University found that people make an average of 226.7 decisions daily about food alone.[1] The more power and responsibility that has been given to us the more complex, difficult, and numerous our decisions become.

King David, for example, was frequently required to make difficult decisions based on the requests that were made of him. Throughout the book of Samuel, we find David using a simple technique that aided his decision-making: asking simple, clarifying questions. Time and again, we find David asking questions such as, "What shall I do for you?" (2 Samuel 21:3) or "What do you want me to do for you?" (v. 4).

At first glance this might seem trivial. After all, who doesn't ask such questions? But when we look closer, we see that David uses such simple questions to collect information for making complex decisions. As the American management expert W. Edwards Deming explained, "The ultimate purpose of taking data is to provide a basis for action or a recommendation."[2] Asking simple questions is often more fruitful in helping us collect the data and clarify our concerns than more complex questions.

**Throughout the book of Samuel, we find David using a simple technique that aided his decision-making: asking simple clarifying questions.**

Imagine, for example, that we feel compelled to change the direction of our spiritual lives. A broad, complex question to ask would be, "What change in my life does God want me to make so I can better serve Him?" A simpler question to ask might be, "What could I do this week to better serve God?"

The simple question helps us to narrow our focus, in this case from the span of a lifetime to a single week. This frees our minds to think about small-scale solutions to our problem. We might decide, for instance, that the best way we could serve this week is to offer to babysit the children of a single mother in our church. This might point us to the larger change we seek to make, such as becoming a foster parent.

Asking simple questions that help us solve small problems ("What do I do this week?") can often help us identify how to answer larger questions ("How should I change my life?").

What are the simple questions you should be asking?

MONTH     DAY     YEAR

GOD SIGHTINGS

## SCRIPTURE I AM MEMORIZING

## WHAT AM I LISTENING TO?

Artist:

Song:

Playlist:

## WHAT IS HAPPENING IN MY LIFE?

## WHAT IS HAPPENING IN THE WORLD?

# How Can I Practice Hospitality?

## READ: 1 KINGS 17:7–24

**The widow at Zarephath** was down to her last meal. Drought had reduced her resources to a handful of flour and a little olive oil, and she expected that she and her son would soon starve. Even if she had wanted to show hospitality by fulfilling Elijah's request for a piece of bread, she couldn't have. She had nothing to give.

Or so she believed. But at his prompting the widow showed hospitality to Elijah anyway, and as he had promised, the "jar of flour was not used up and the jug of oil did not run dry" (1 Kings 17:16).

The widow's story provides us with one of the fundamental ways of practicing hospitality: simply share what you have. Our meals might be modest, but we can share them in a spirit of generosity and love. And if our hospitality is directed toward those who cannot repay us (Luke 14:13–14), then it shouldn't matter. To those who have nothing to eat, any meal can be a feast.

> The widow's story provides us with one of the fundamental ways of practicing hospitality: simply share what you have.

Along with that primary rule—simply share what you have—keep in mind these three realities when practicing hospitality:

Hospitality must be offered without grumbling: Peter made it unmistakably clear: offer hospitality to one another without grumbling (1 Peter 4:9).

1.  Hospitality is not the same as *entertaining*: Entertaining (providing amusement or enjoyment, such as at a dinner party) has little to do with real hospitality if the goal is to impress others rather than to serve, says Trisha Wilkerson: Entertaining says, "I want to impress you with my beautiful home, my clever decorating, my gourmet cooking." Hospitality, however, seeks to minister. It says, "This home is not mine. It is truly a gift from my Master. I am his servant, and I use it as he desires."[1]

2.  Hospitality is not without risk: With the crucifixion of Jesus, the world displayed the ultimate betrayal of the hospitality shown to us by God. Since that was the way we treated the most perfect Host, we shouldn't be surprised when the practice of hospitality proves costly. "We are not above our master," says Jonathan R. Wilson. "Like him we will endure suffering, persecution, and even death as we learn love through the practice of hospitality."[2]

List the ways you will be more hospitable in the future.

GOD SIGHTINGS

SCRIPTURE I AM MEMORIZING

WHAT AM I LISTENING TO?

Artist:

Song:

Playlist:

WHAT IS HAPPENING IN MY LIFE?

WHAT IS HAPPENING IN THE WORLD?

# How Can I Develop Humility?

## READ: 2 CHRONICLES 7:14

**After the dedication of the temple,** God appears to Solomon at night and tells him that if the people "will humble themselves and pray and seek my face and turn from their wicked ways, then I will hear from heaven, and I will forgive their sin and will heal their land" (2 Chronicles 7:14).

We know we need to humble ourselves before God. But what does that mean, and what does it require? Let's look at some of the ways we can develop humility:

> We fail to humble ourselves when we develop an inaccurate view of ourselves.

- Fight pride and self-doubt: Humility allows us to see ourselves in proper relation to God and neighbor, leading us to an accurate self-assessment. We fail to humble ourselves when we develop an inaccurate view of ourselves because of either pride or self-doubt—both enemies of humility that we must battle. As Greg Willson explains, Pride and self-doubt are really two sides of the same coin. One believes that we know better than God does; the other believes that He isn't good or powerful enough to change us. Neither makes much of God, effectively bringing Him down below us. The prideful and the self-doubters both believe they're better than God; they just show it in different ways.[1]

- Use truth as the primary tool: The primary means we humble ourselves is by learning what God has to say about us. When you search Scripture, make note of all the things—both positive and negative—God has to say about mankind. Only by learning God's truth can we acquire the self-knowledge necessary to develop humility.

- Surround yourself with people who will exhort and rebuke you: We need people in our lives who will provide an honest assessment—praising us for our virtues and chastising us for our failings.

- Serve others: Humility is not just about agreeing to an idea of who we are, but rather it is self-knowledge gained through experience. The surest way to gain such experiential knowledge is by serving others (Galatians 5:13). Through service, we learn that our God-given talents and abilities make us different, but not better, than our neighbor.

How can you apply the applications and lessons about humility in
2 Chronicles 7:14 to your life?

GOD SIGHTINGS

SCRIPTURE I AM MEMORIZING

WHAT AM I LISTENING TO?

Artist:

Song:

Playlist:

WHAT IS HAPPENING IN MY LIFE?

WHAT IS HAPPENING IN THE WORLD?

# SECTION 17

# How Can My Grace Create Integrity?

## READ: PSALM 26:1

**In his *Confessions*,** Augustine says that as a young man he prayed, "Grant me chastity and continence, but not yet." He worried that God would "hear me too soon and too soon cure me of my disease of lust."[1] In other words, Augustine did not want to have his sinful desires removed, but to satisfy his lust.

Young Augustine knew the value of integrity (the quality of having strong moral principles), but thought it was something he could obtain later in life. Unfortunately, we are often tempted to pray a similar prayer: "Grant me sanctification, but not yet."

We get this attitude when we misunderstand God's grace. As Jeremy Treat explains, we have a misconception that grace gives us permission to sin:

> If God graciously forgives sin, then why struggle for a sin-free life? "I'm good at sinning, God is good at forgiving; it's a match made in heaven, right?" This common mindset presumes that it's God's job to forgive our sin. He's God—that's just what he does. But the minute we presume upon grace, it is no longer grace. *Grace is not permission to sin, it*

95

*is the power to overcome sin.* By grace God forgives sin *and* transforms sinners into saints. Holiness is not a prerequisite for grace; it is a product of grace.[2]

Compare this attitude to David, who said, "Vindicate me, Lord, for I have led a blameless life; I have trusted in the Lord and have not faltered" (Psalm 26:1).

David didn't claim he led a perfect life, only that he's maintained a purity of heart and honesty of the soul because of his unwavering trust in God.[3] He was consistent in his character from the time of his youth because he understood the value of God's grace.

David shows us it's not only important to be a person of integrity in the future, but that we must maintain our integrity over time. If we do not intend to be the type of person who would live a life of sin in the *future*, then we should not live a life of sin *today*.

How has someone extended grace to you? Have you recently extended grace to someone? How has grace changed your mindset?

MONTH      DAY      YEAR

GOD SIGHTINGS

SCRIPTURE I AM MEMORIZING

WHAT AM I LISTENING TO?

Artist:

Song:

Playlist:

WHAT IS HAPPENING IN MY LIFE?

WHAT IS HAPPENING IN THE WORLD?

# How Can I Develop Self-Control?

## READ: PROVERBS 25:28

**From ancient times** to the medieval period, defensive walls were a city's primary defense against outside aggressors. Beyond their defensive utility, though, many walls also had important symbolic functions because they represented the status and independence of the communities they embraced.[1] Both of those uses should be reflected in our reading of Proverbs 25:28: "Like a city whose walls are broken through is a person who lacks self-control." Lack of self-control makes us vulnerable to outside evils, threatens our reputation and status, and takes away our independence.

The characteristic most closely related to self-control is conscientiousness. Conscientiousness refers to the type of impulse control that facilitates task- and goal-oriented behaviors, such as thinking before acting, delaying gratification, following rules, planning, organizing, and prioritizing tasks.[2] Social scientists

> **Lack of self-control makes us vulnerable to outside evils, threatens our reputation and status, and takes away our independence.**

have shown that conscientiousness is the only major personality trait that consistently leads to success in worldly endeavors.[3]

Here are three mini-habits that can help us improve conscientiousness and develop self-control:

1. Spend one minute at a set time every day asking God to increase your conscientiousness.
2. Memorize and meditate on 2 Timothy 1:7: "For the Spirit God gave us does not make us timid, but gives us power, love and self-discipline."
3. Make a list of all the times you can think of over the past few months when you have shown a lack of self-control. Identify the possible "triggers" (events, people, moods) that preceded your actions. Write down what you can do differently to change such situations in the future.

MONTH    DAY    YEAR

GOD SIGHTINGS

SCRIPTURE I AM MEMORIZING

WHAT AM I LISTENING TO?

Artist:

Song:

Playlist:

WHAT IS HAPPENING IN MY LIFE?

WHAT IS HAPPENING IN THE WORLD?

# How Can I Participate in God's Work?

## READ: ECCLESIASTES 5:18-20

**The teacher in Ecclesiastes** 5:18 said, "This is what I have observed to be good: that it is appropriate for a person to eat, to drink and to find satisfaction in their toilsome labor under the sun during the few days of life God has given them—for this is their lot."

"Toilsome labor" is work that is incessant, extremely hard, or exhausting. That doesn't sound all that appealing, so why does Solomon say it's "good"? Because, he adds, "to accept their lot and be happy in their toil—this is a gift of God. They seldom reflect on the days of their life, because God keeps them occupied with gladness of heart" (vv. 19–20).

One of the reasons we can be "happy in our toil" and do so with "gladness of heart" is by recognizing that through our labors we are participating in God's own work. As Amy L. Sherman says,

> Work is not evil, nor is it a side effect of sin. This truth can be hard for congregants to trust when they are frustrated in their jobs or unfulfilled in their careers. It's certainly true that the curse of Genesis 3 brought toil and futility into work. Ever since, our experience of work involves pain as well as pleasure. But work itself is good. It has intrinsic value.[1]

Our labor has intrinsic value because, as Sherman adds, we are "made in the image of God, and God is a worker." God also uses our labors to serve the needs of our neighbors. In fact, for most of us, the labor we are engaged in during our jobs is the primary way we serve our neighbors.

God should be our "vocational model," says Robert Banks. Banks describes the various sorts of work God does and how, through our own vocations, we can imitate God's work:[2]

- Redemptive work (God's saving and reconciling actions): This is work we often associate with ministry (pastors, evangelists, counselors), though it can also include occupations such as artists, writers, and songwriters who incorporate redemptive elements into their creative productions.
- Creative work (God's fashioning of the physical and human world): While only God can create something out of nothing," says Art Lindsley, "we can create something from something—and are called to this creative task."[3] "Sub-creators" was the favorite term of J. R. R. Tolkien and Francis Schaeffer to describe this type of work. But other scholars, Lindsley notes, use the term "co-creators," indicating we participate with God in creative acts. Such workers include artists of various types (musicians, poets, sculptors), craftspeople (carpenters, bricklayers,

metalworkers) and those who design (architects, fashion designers, urban planners).

• Providential work (God's provision for and sustaining of humans and the creation): "The work of divine providence includes all that God does to maintain the universe and human life in an orderly and beneficial fashion," says Banks. "This includes conserving, sustaining, and replenishing, in addition to creating and redeeming the world." Almost any job that creates or maintains order can fall into this category. Creating and maintaining order is a role under many spheres, such as government (politicians, public utility workers, city clerks), public safety (firefighters, police officers), environmental (custodians, cleaners, garbage collectors), and economic (statisticians, economists, shopkeepers).

• Justice work (God's maintenance of justice): Judges, lawyers, paralegals, government regulators, legal secretaries, city managers, prison wardens and guards, diplomats, and law enforcement personnel participate in God's work of maintaining justice, notes Sherman.[4]

• Compassionate work (God's involvement in comforting, healing, guiding, and shepherding): Roles that reflect this aspect of God's labor include doctors, nurses, paramedics, psychologists, therapists, social workers, pharmacists, community workers, nonprofit directors, emergency medical technicians, and counselors.

• Revelatory work (God's work to enlighten with truth): Teachers, scientists, journalists, scholars, and most writers are involved in this type of labor.

A key step in being "happy in our toil" is to recognize which vocation model our work most reflects. Which category does your own job fall into? Reflect on how God uses your work to imitate His own.

MONTH    DAY    YEAR

GOD SIGHTINGS

SCRIPTURE I AM MEMORIZING

WHAT AM I LISTENING TO?

Artist:

Song:

Playlist:

WHAT IS HAPPENING IN MY LIFE?

WHAT IS HAPPENING IN THE WORLD?

# How Do I Praise God's Attributes?

## READ: ISAIAH 63:7

**In the Bible,** praise is the celebration, honoring, and adoration of God in the power of the Holy Spirit, whether by an individual believer or by a community of believers.[1]

Although prayer is not the same as praise, they are usually tied together, as in Isaiah 63:7:

> I will tell of the kindnesses of the LORD,
> the deeds for which he is to be praised,
> according to all the LORD has done for us—
> yes, the many good things
> he has done for Israel,
> according to his compassion and many kindnesses.

"Prayer and praise," said Charles Spurgeon, "are like the two cherubim on the ark, they must never be separated."[2] Praise is not for God's benefit—for in His perfection He lacks nothing—but for our own. By giving praise for His attributes, we are better able to recognize and respond to a holy God.

Here, then, are four ways you can praise God's attributes in your prayers:

**1** Identify God's attributes: Make a list of thirty-one attributes of God, then list a Scripture verse that talks about that quality. For example, you could note that God is compassionate and gracious (Exodus 34:6–7). For one month, select one attribute a day to focus on in your prayer.

**2** Reflect on the attribute: Too often we talk about qualities without truly thinking about what they mean. This is especially true when we talk about the attributes of God. Before you pray, look up the meaning of that attribute in a reference, such as a theological dictionary.

**3** Praise that attribute in your prayer: Begin your prayer by praising God for the particular attribute you've chosen to focus on that day. If applicable, mention examples from your own life. For example, "I praise You, Lord, for Your compassion and graciousness. Thank You for the compassion You showed to me when . . ."

**4** Create a list of "praise prompts" Contemplate the following list of Praise Prompt Starters, and use the ones that move you:

- God the Creator—I praise You, God, because "You alone are the Lord. You made the heavens, even the highest heavens, and all their starry host, the earth and all that is on it, the seas and all that is in them. You give life to everything, and the multitudes of heaven worship you" (Nehemiah 9:6).
- God the only Lord—I praise You, God, because you are "the Lord, and there is no other; apart from [you] there is no God" (Isaiah 45:5).
- God the Almighty—I praise You, God, because "who is like you,

Lord God Almighty? You, Lord, are mighty, and your faithfulness surrounds you" (Psalm 89:8).

- God the Prince of Peace—I praise You, God, my "Wonderful Counselor, Mighty God, Everlasting Father, Prince of Peace" (Isaiah 9:6).
- God, whose nature is love—I praise You, God, because "God is love. Whoever lives in love lives in God, and God in them" (1 John 4:16).
- God the triumphant—I praise You, God, "who always leads us as captives in Christ's triumphal procession and uses us to spread the aroma of the knowledge of him everywhere" (2 Corinthians 2:14).
- God the faithful—I praise You, God, for You keep your covenant of love to a thousand generations of those who love You and keep Your commandments (See Deuteronomy 7:9).
- God our refuge—I praise You, God, because my salvation and my honor depend on You, oh God; You are "my mighty rock, my refuge" (Psalm 62:7).
- God, the performer of miracles—I praise You, God, for "you are the God who performs miracles; you display your power among all the peoples" (Psalm 77:14).
- God the Deliverer—I praise You, God, for though I am poor and needy you are my help and my deliverer (Psalm 70:5).

Add to this list by creating your own list of "praise prompts" that you can use in future prayers.

MONTH    DAY    YEAR

GOD SIGHTINGS

SCRIPTURE I AM MEMORIZING

WHAT AM I LISTENING TO?

Artist:

Song:

Playlist:

WHAT IS HAPPENING IN MY LIFE?

WHAT IS HAPPENING IN THE WORLD?

# Notes

**SECTION 1**

1. Walter A. Elwell and Barry J. Beitzel, "Obedience," *Baker Encyclopedia of the Bible,* ed. Walter A. Elwell (Grand Rapids, MI: Baker, 1988).
2. Rod Loy, *Immediate Obedience* (Springfield, MO: Influence Resources, 2014).

**SECTION 2**

1. Kurt Strassner, *Opening Up Genesis* (London: Day One Publications, 2009).

**SECTION 3**

1. Aaron Sironi, "From Your Heart . . . Forgive," *The Journal of Biblical Counseling* 26, no.3 (2012). http://www.ccef.org/sites/default/files/journal-articles/From-Your-Heart-Forgive.pdf.
2. Rose Sweet, "Why Do We Find It So Hard to Forgive?" Focus on the Family, accessed February 23, 2015, http://www.focusonthefamily.com/marriage/divorce-and-infidelity /forgiveness-and-restoration/forgiveness-what-it-is-and-what-it-isnt.
3. Ibid.
4. Sironi, "From Your Heart . . . Forgive."

**SECTION 4**

1. Charles Duhigg, *The Power of Habit* (New York: Random House, 2011).

**SECTION 5**

1. John Piper, "The Law of Christ," *Desiring God*, August 14, 1983, http://www.desiringgod .org/sermons/the-law-of-christ.
2. Tim Challies, "An Extraordinary Skill for Ordinary Christians," Challies.com, February 16, 2015, http://www.challies.com/christian-living/an-extraordinary-skill-for-ordinarychristians.

## SECTION 6

1. Timothy Keller, "How to Find Your Rival Gods," *Christianity Today,* October 20, 2009, http://www.christianitytoday.com/ct/2009/octoberweb-only/142–21.0.html.

## SECTION 7

1. Duhigg, *The Power of Habit.*

## SECTION 8

1. R. Dennis Cole, Numbers: *An Exegetical and Theological Exposition of Holy Scripture (The New American Commentary)*, vol. 3B (Nashville: Broadman & Holman, 2000).

## SECTION 9

1. Cole, "Numbers."
2. "What were the cities of refuge in the Old Testament?" Got Questions Ministries, accessed December 1, 2014, http://www.gotquestions.org/cities-of-refuge.html.

## SECTION 10

1. Ruth Haley Barton, "Solitude," in *Dictionary of Christian Spirituality*, ed. Glen G. Scorgie (Grand Rapids, MI: Zondervan, 2011).

## SECTION 11

1. Daniel Isaac Block, *Judges, Ruth: An Exegetical and Theological Exposition of Holy Scripture (The New American Commentary)*, vol. 6 (Nashville: Broadman & Holman, 1999).
2. C. S. Lewis, *The Four Loves* (Chicago: Mariner Books, 1971).
3. Joseph Rhea, "Why the Church Needs Intergenerational Friendships," The Gospel Coalition, January 8, 2015, http://www.thegospelcoalition.org/article/why-the -churchneeds-intergenerational-friendships.

## SECTION 12

1. Joe M. Sprinkle, "Law," *Evangelical Dictionary of Theology* ed. Walter A. Elwell (Grand Rapids, MI: Baker, 1996), 467.
2. Justin Taylor, "A Primer on the Mosaic Law and the Christian," The Gospel Coalition, September 13, 2006, http://www.thegospelcoalition.org/blogs/justintaylor/2006/09/13 /primer-on-mosaic-law-and-christian/.

## SECTION 13

1. Garrett Kell, "Giving and Receiving Godly Criticism: Sharpening Each Other With Your Words," *9Marks*, February 3, 2015, http://9marks.org/article/giving-and-receivinggodly-criticism-sharpening-each-other-with-your-words/.
2. Ibid.

## SECTION 14

1. Ibid.
2. Jon Bloom, "The Priceless Grace of Pressure," *DesiringGod*, August 8, 2014, http://www.desiringgod.org/articles/the-priceless-grace-of-pressure.

## SECTION 15

1. Trisha Wilkerson, *Everyday Worship: Our Work, Heart and Jesus* (Scotland: Christian Focus, 2013).
2. Jonathan R. Wilson, *Gospel Virtues: Practicing Faith, Hope, and Love in Uncertain Times* (London: Wipf & Stock, 2004).

## SECTION 16

1. Greg Willson, "The Prideful Pursuit of Humility," *Gospel-Centered Discipleship*, accessed February 3, 2015, http://gcdiscipleship.com/the-prideful-pursuit-of-humility.

## SECTION 17

1. Augustine, *Confessions*, accessed February 4, 2015, http://www.gutenberg.org/files/3296/3296-h/3296-h.htm.
2. Jeremy Treat, "Grace Is Not a Thing," The Gospel Coalition, May 29, 2014, http://www.thegospelcoalition.org/article/grace-is-not-a-thing.
3. John Peter Lange et al., *A Commentary on the Holy Scriptures: Psalms* (New York: Ulan Press, 2008).

## SECTION 18

1. "Defensive Wall," *Wikipedia*, accessed December 20, 2014, http://en.wikipedia.org/wiki/Defensive_wall.
2. Lawrence A. Pervin and P. John Olivers, eds., *Handbook of Personality: Theory and Research* (New York: Guilford Press, 1999).
3. Drake Baer, "Science Says This Personality Trait Predicts Job Performance," *Business Insider*, December 19, 2014, http://www.businessinsider.com/conscientiousnesspredicts-job-performance–2014–12.

## SECTION 19

1. Amy L. Sherman, *Kingdom Calling: Vocational Stewardship for the Common Good* (Downers Grove, IL: InterVarsity Press, 2011).

2. Robert Banks, *Faith Goes to Work: Reflections from the Marketplace* (London: Wipf & Stock, 1999), 38.

3. Art Lindsley, "The Call to Creativity: What's Dignity Got to Do with It?" *Institute for Faith, Work, and Economics,* October 25, 2012, http://blog.tifwe.org/the-call-tocreativity-whats-dignity-got-to-do-with-it/.

4. Sherman, *Kingdom Calling.*

## SECTION 20

1. Martin H. Manser, *Dictionary of Bible Themes: The Accessible and Comprehensive Tool for Topical Studies* (London: Hodder & Stoughton, 2009).

2. Charles Spurgeon, "Prayer Perfumed with Praise," *The Spurgeon Archive,* accessed December 29, 2014, http://www.spurgeon.org/sermons/1469.htm.